W9-BGZ-855

Easter

Julie Murray

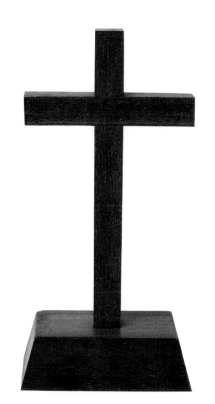

Abdo
HOLIDAYS
Kids

abdopublishing.com

Published by Abdo Kids, a division of ABDO, PO Box 398166, Minneapolis, Minnesota 55439.
Copyright © 2018 by Abdo Consulting Group, Inc. International copyrights reserved in all countries.
No part of this book may be reproduced in any form without written permission from the publisher.

Printed in the United States of America, North Mankato, Minnesota.

102017

012018

 THIS BOOK CONTAINS
RECYCLED MATERIALS

Photo Credits: Glow Images, iStock, Shutterstock

Production Contributors: Teddy Borth, Jennie Forsberg, Grace Hansen

Design Contributors: Christina Doffing, Candice Keimig, Dorothy Toth

Publisher's Cataloging in Publication Data

Names: Murray, Julie, author.

Title: Easter / by Julie Murray.

Description: Minneapolis, Minnesota : Abdo Kids, 2018. | Series: Holidays |
        Includes glossary, index and online resource (page 24).

Identifiers: LCCN 2017942861 | ISBN 9781532103933 (lib.bdg.) | ISBN 9781532105050 (ebook) |
        ISBN 9781532105616 (Read-to-me ebook)

Subjects: LCSH: Holidays--Juvenile literature. | Easter--Juvenile literature. |
        Christian Holiday--Juvenile literature. | Spiritual holiday--Juvenile literature.

Classification: DDC 394.2667--dc23

LC record available at https://lccn.loc.gov/2017942861

Table of Contents

Easter

Easter is about new life. It is in the spring.

Spring is full of new life.
Flowers grow. Many baby
animals are born.

Christians celebrate Easter.

They believe Jesus rose

from the dead.

Max goes to church. He learns about Jesus.

Families get together. They share a **special** meal.

Nan looks in her basket.

The eggs are full of candy!

15

Jan paints eggs. She likes
the polka dots!

Cara finds an egg. She puts

it in her basket.

Tom loves Easter!

Signs of Easter

Easter basket

Easter bunny

Easter eggs

Jesus

22

Glossary

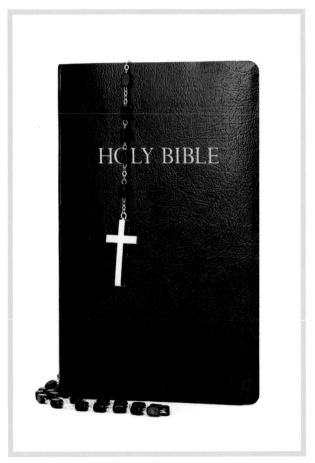

Christian
a member of the Christian church who believes in Jesus Christ and follows his words and teachings.

special
out of the ordinary.

Index

Abdo Kids ONLINE
FREE! ONLINE MULTIMEDIA RESOURCES

Visit **abdokids.com** and use this code to access crafts, games, videos, and more!

Abdo Kids Code:
HEK3933